MANNHEIM STEAMROLLER
A FRESH AIRE *Christmas*

ARRANGED BY: CHIP DAVIS
Solo Piano Reduction and Editing by Jackson Berkey,
featured Keyboardist with Mannheim Steamroller.

*Full score and parts available for keyboards,
choir and orchestra for "Traditions of Christmas"
and "Veni, Veni."*

*Contact American Gramaphone Records for
details 402-457-4341*

Published by Dots and Lines Ink*
9130 Mormon Bridge Road Omaha, Ne. 68152

*except where noted

MANNHEIM STEAMROLLER
A FRESH AIRE Christmas

Hark! The Herald Angels Sing

Arranged by Chip Davis

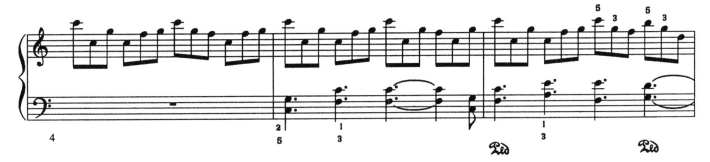

46

49

52

55

58 pedal as before

76

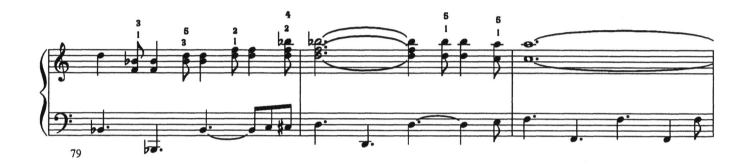

79

82

85

88

91

94

97

100

103

Veni, Veni
(O Come, O Come Emmanuel)

Arranged by Chip Davis

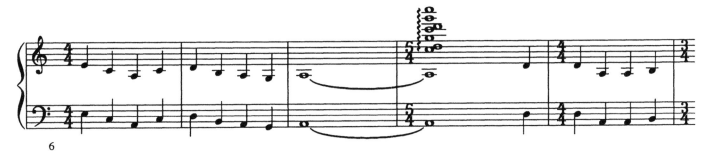

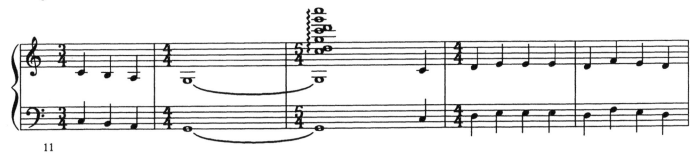

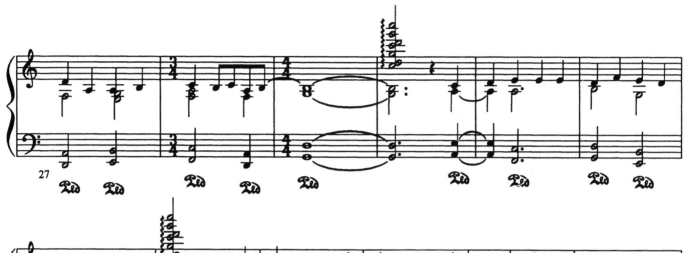

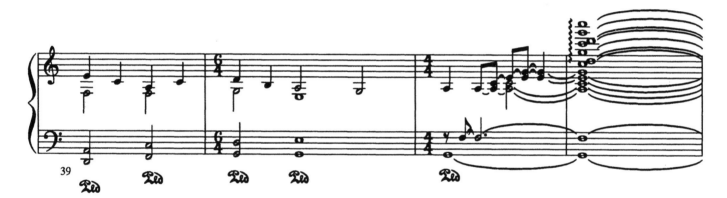

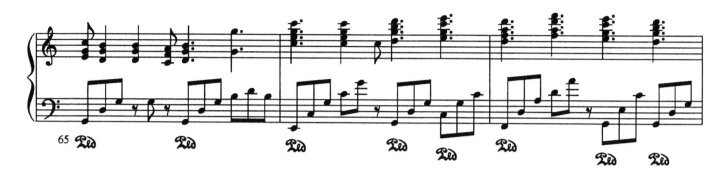

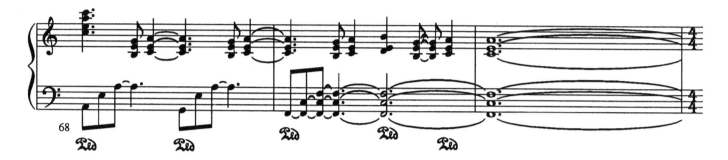

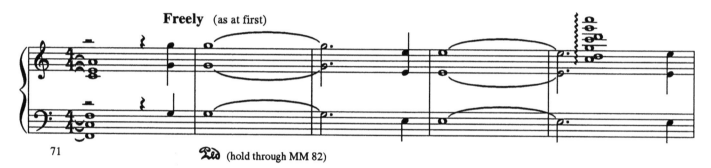

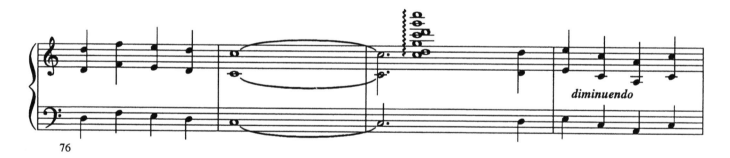

The Holly and the Ivy

Arranged by Chip Davis

Little Drummer Boy

Arranged by Chip Davis

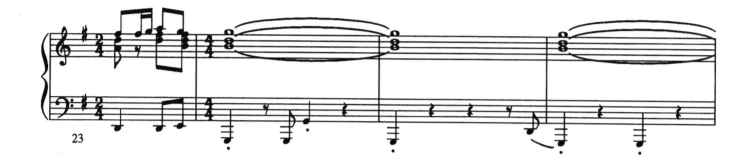

sempre **f** *e in tempo*   *al fine*

Still, Still, Still

Very sustained throughout   (♩ = 64)

Rearranged by Chip Davis

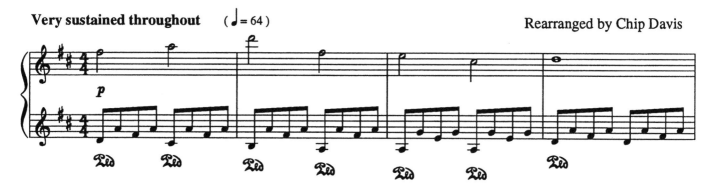

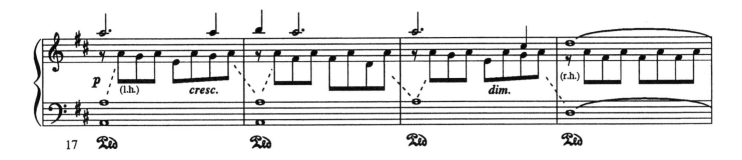

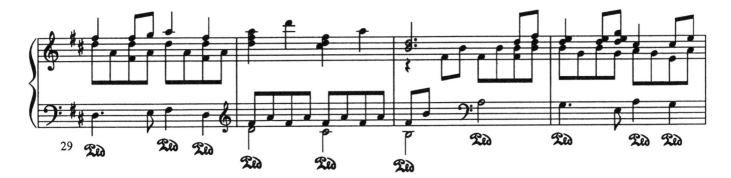

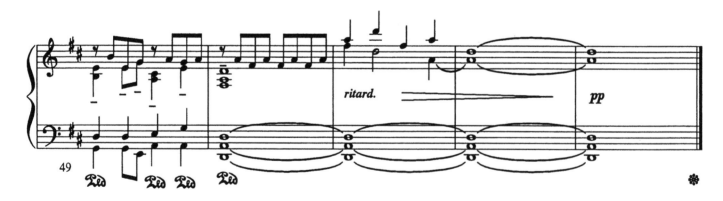

Lo, How a Rose E'er Blooming

Arranged by Chip Davis

23

(accentuate melody)

27

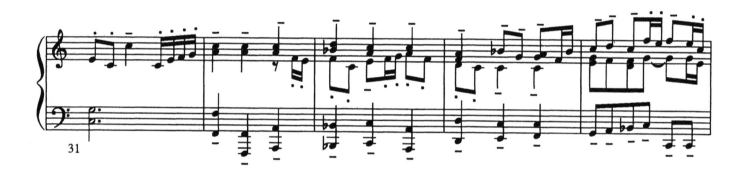

31

36

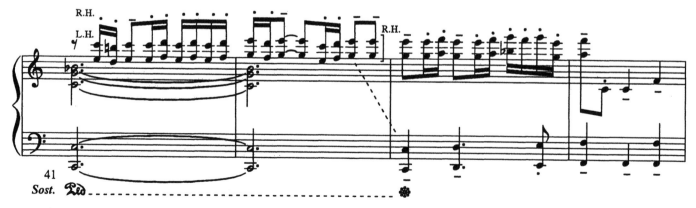

R.H.

L.H.

R.H.

41

Sost. Ped --------------------------------- ✻

In Dulci Jubilo

Arranged by Chip Davis

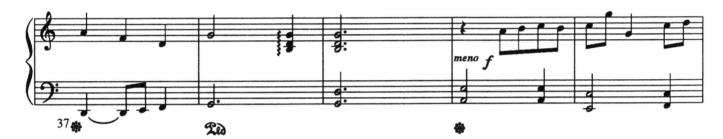

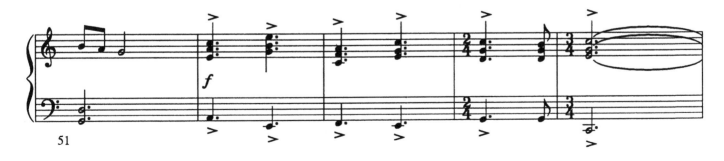

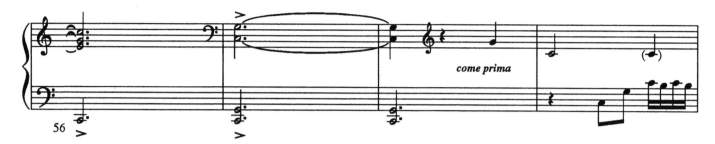

come prima

113

(like harpsichord)

117

122

Sost.

127

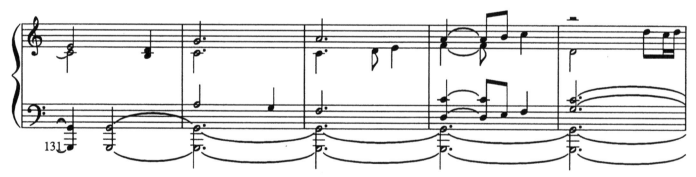

131

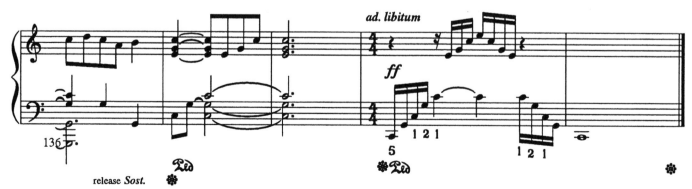

ad. libitum

ff

5   1 2 1   1 2 1

136

release Sost.

Greensleeves

Arranged by Chip Davis

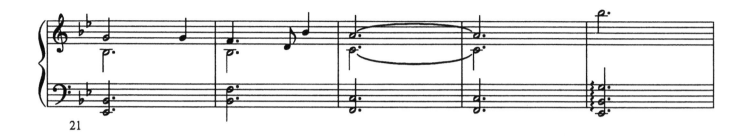

21

26

31

36

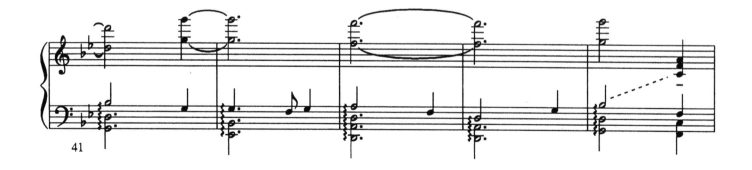

41

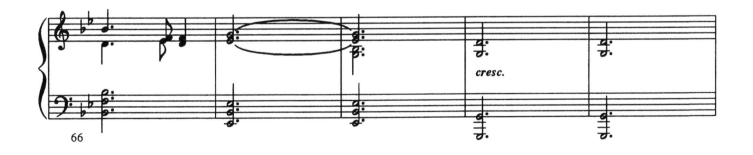

71

76

81

86

91

96

101

Carol of the Bells

Arranged by Chip Davis

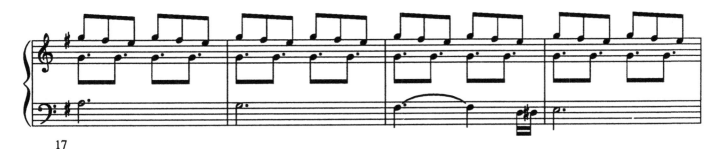

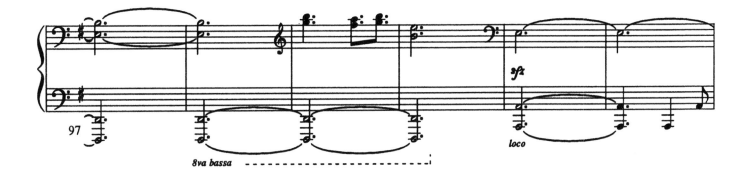

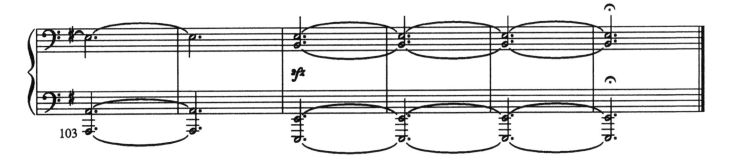

Traditions of Christmas

Original carol by Chip Davis

Cantique de Noël
(O Holy Night)

Arranged by Chip Davis

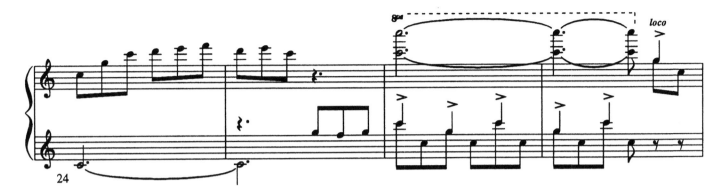

47

51

56

61 (melody)

66

71

(melody)

75

(melody)

80

85

ff

89

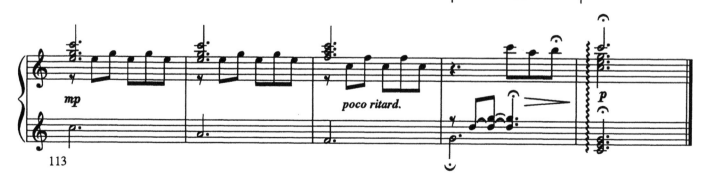

HARK! THE HERALD ANGELS SING
18th Century German

In the tradition of "Deck the Halls" from the first Christmas album, this cut was to bring back memories of how you felt the first time you heard Mannheim Steamroller Christmas. And...of course...for fun.

VENI VENI (O COME O COME EMANUEL)
12th Century French

When I decided to arrange this, I started looking for an unusual way to go about this arrangement. The melody really reminds me of a Gregorian chant and I thought that would be very unusual to hear on a Christmas album. It also seemed neat to accompany the chant with handbells (which we borrowed from Grace Bible Institute). After driving my assistant, Brian, nuts for about two weeks sampling the wave forms and editing durations, we finally loaded the handbells into the sampler to be played in a very polyphonic way, uncharacteristic to handbells.

As for a choir, to sing Veni Veni, I thought the purity of the Cambridge singers with "cathedral echo" seemed most appropriate. As the arrangement and performance mediums got more unusual, I decided to do the most unusual of all... translate it to Latin. That would really make it unusual, so in arranging the choral session, I asked my friend John Rutter if he knew of anyone who could translate "O Come O Come Emanuel" to Latin to add to this unusual approach. He said, "Oh, it's already in Latin; in fact, it was written in Latin because it was originally a Gregorian chant." And was probably performed with handbells? So much for my unusual approach.

THE HOLLY & THE IVY
Ancient French Melody

From an Old French carol of ancient times. The Holly and the Ivy were symbolic of the ancient worship of nature. This carol became yet another blending of a secular topic with a sacred topic.

LITTLE DRUMMER BOY
20th Century American

Of course being a drummer myself, I sought this tune, not only because of its popularity, but it was one I could really have fun with. I envisioned this as a toy soldier being built in Santa's Workshop and being fitted with a drum instead of a rifle. The piece progresses from synthetic to acoustic as did my image of the drummer, turning from a toy to a real person.

STILL, STILL, STILL
Austrian Carol

Still, Still, Still is an Austrian carol. This arrangement is based on the arrangement, known by choirs world over, by Norman Luboff. Every year for 15 years my father ended his Christmas concert with Still, Still, Still. I grew up with this piece and after college went to work for Norman Luboff as a singer. This is where I met Jackson Berkey who plays keyboards on all of these recordings. Norman passed on last year and I wanted to add this as a reminder of the wonderful musical gifts he left on this earth, and for all the musicians he inspired. John Rutter, Jackson and I were very close to Norman and I know I speak for all when I say how much we miss him.

LO HOW A ROSE E'ER BLOOMING
15th Century German

This carol is 15th century German, also in the antiphonal treatment, this setting is a play between two composers' styles. The chorale version I used is the harmonization by Michael Praetorius done in the year 1609.

Most people are more familiar with the Bach harmonization, so I used the older Praetorius but treated my harmonization in the style of Bach.

1609 was the year Kepler wrote his treatis called "The Dream" on space travel. This was the topic of Fresh Aire V. Just another weird collision in time.

IN DULCI JUBILO
16th Century German

In the tradition of the first Mannheim Steamroller Christmas, I thought it only appropriate that at least one carol be done in the style of the Renaissance to carry on the concept of "Christmas Sweet."

This carol comes from a legend about a German monk who lived in 1365 named Heinrich Suso. This carol was one to start a tradition of blending secular and sacred. Latin, being the language of the church, was often interspersed with the mother tongue. Hence, the title.

GREENSLEEVES

16th Century English

Because of the staggering number of requests for
this, I decided to do it again (fourth time) for
this album. It shows up on several other albums
in the American Gramaphone catalog. This is an
Old English folk song from around the time of
Shakespeare. I saved the beauty of the entirety of
the tune until the last of the arrangement as not
to wear out its charm.

CAROL OF THE BELLS

19th Century Ukrainian

Carol of the Bells is a Ukrainian carol written in the
19th century. This piece is very repetitive and it
presented a real challenge from an arranging stand-
point. Without the benefit of words to change each
verse, there was only about 20 seconds of music to
work with. Also, this piece is in the minor mode and
can become very dark. I lightened it up by writing
one third of it in the major mode.

I built the arrangement on the rhythm pattern of
the melody which, in "musician talk" takes on the
characteristic of a pattern called 2 against 3.

The melody and many parts are played by all
kinds of bells—handbells, synthetic bells, tubular
bells, etc.

TRADITIONS OF CHRISTMAS

Chip Davis 1988

As many of you who are on our mailing list know,
this album was chosen by the fans through sending in
request postcards. I had toyed with writing a Christmas carol myself anyway, but when the votes came
in, to my surprise, I only got one vote so...why do
an original? I felt so sorry for myself, I decided to
do it for that one person. This is all about fuzzy
warm sweaters, soft images of the tree, cookies in
the oven on Christmas morning and family.

It was you, wasn't it...Sharon.

CANTIQUE DE NOEL
(O HOLY NIGHT)

19th Century French

This carol was composed by Adolphe Adam in the
early to mid 1800's. People all over Paris would
come to the large churches at Christmas time to
hear the "Cantique de Noel." Since this piece is
from around the time of Beethoven, I gave it a little
Beethoven in the introduction with the melody
in the bass.